MW00618616

THE
LEADERSHIP MINDSET
WEEKLY

THE ART AND SCIENCE
OF
MOVING POSSIBILITY INTO REALITY

*52 WEEKLY PRACTICES TO TRANSFORM
YOUR LEADERSHIP MINDSET*

Blaine Bartlett

A Soul of Business™
Publication

GLENMOORE
PRESS

Greenbank, Washington
U.S.A

ISBN: 978-0-9776656-6-2
ISBN: 978-0-9776656-7-9

CONTENT

INTRODUCTION

How important are the lessons you will be working with in this book? Consider this: *There is nothing on this planet that is not touched in some way by the activity of leadership.* Business and its activity are the most pervasive and prevalent force on the planet today. How our lives and businesses are led and managed literally determines the wealth, health and well-being of everything and everyone on our planet. With this in mind it becomes incumbent on the leaders of businesses to ensure that the activities of their organizations are structured in ways that follow the admonishment of Hippocrates to "first do no harm." The fact that this is not the focus of most organizations poses a considerable challenge to leaders who aspire to inspire others and to do good works. It's a challenge that is reinforced because many business leaders don't pay particular attention to how they are leading themselves!

One of Henry David Thoreau's most frequently quoted sayings is "The mass of men lead lives of quiet desperation." The paradox with this profound observation is that his friend and mentor, Ralph Waldo Emerson, thought that if his protégé had one flaw, it was a lack of ambition. So, what then may Thoreau have been alluding to? Simply this, heeding unquestioningly the call of "success" as society and culture would define it is a sure way to lose oneself. Ambition for what and ambition to what end were questions that Thoreau thought worthy of exploration. His experiment in self-reliance as captured in his book *Walden Pond* was essentially a proof of the power of one's mindset to either obscure or illuminate possibilities. In the course of his time at Walden Pond he wrote many things concerning these questions.

As noted by authors Brett and Kate McKay when writing about Thoreau: "When you genuinely feel that the things within your own spirit, and in your own backyard, are enough to bring you boundless joy and excitement, when you're able to be by yourself without being bored, then you have the power to pursue ambitious goals without being tempted to compromise your principles to obtain them. You'll have the power to work only to cover necessities, and/or because you enjoy it, rather than as a route to more possessions or worldly status. You'll have the power to step off the treadmill of desire and feel the inherently rich abundance with which you're already surrounded."

"When you're able to be by yourself without being bored..." This then is the purpose of this book and the importance of the lessons that follow. As Thoreau himself noted, "...the cost of a thing is the amount of what I will call life, which is required to be exchanged for it, immediately or in the long run." In his book *Henry Thoreau: A Life of the Mind,* Robert D. Richardson says about Thoreau, when a man acts on his convictions, even in the smallest ways, "the contagion of his example unhinges the universe."

Over the course of the weekly lessons that make up this book 'll be visiting with leaders, sages, philosophers and wise men and women who have explored questions of authenticity, truth, power, and relationship – all in service of answering the question of how to be more effective as a leader and as a human being.

The weekly lessons you'll explore are organized in alignment with the definition leadership as being the activity of *co-creating coordinated movement*. Einstein once said that "nothing happens until something moves." Action is required in order to co-create coordinated movement and the acronym **ACCCT** (**A**wareness, **C**ontext, **C**ommunication mastery, **C**ommitment, **T**rust) is my shorthand for the key elements that comprise this very specific kind of action. Leaders act to cause movement. In order to create sustainable success in life that action needs to be intentional and disciplined. A dedicated study of the lessons in this small book can transform the way you lead your life and your organization.

To help you accelerate and deepen your integration of the lessons and practices you'll find in this book you can also join the dedicated **LEADERSHIP MINDSET MASTERMIND** at:

https://Learn.BlaineBartlett.com/lmm

PART 1

The DOMAIN

of

AWARENESS

Month 1

AWARENESS

~ CONSCIOUSNESS ~

"Man's chief delusion is his conviction that there are causes other than his own state of consciousness. All that befalls a man, all that is done by him, all that comes from him, happens as a result of his state of consciousness. A man's consciousness is all that he thinks and desires and loves, all that he believes is true and consents to. That is why a change of consciousness is necessary before you can change your outer world."

~ Neville Goddard, *The Power of Awareness*

It is literally not an exaggeration to claim that there is no one and no thing "out there" except me. What limits my performance and my experience of life, leadership, love, success and money is who I think and believe I am *not*. In order to have, do and be more I need to expand my comfort zone. Learning and growth are always accompanied by discomfort.

Effective leadership is definitely not for the faint of heart. It requires courage and discipline. As a leader I am called on to move into the unknown, to go places I'm not certain of and that others fear to tread. Not foolishly...but with discernment and a clear understanding of the "for the sake of what" I am undertaking this journey.

Awareness is the great enabler. The power of awareness is that an increase in awareness makes visible choices that weren't previously obvious. My willingness and ability to act on and with these now visible choices is what is meant by being limited by who I think I'm not. "I'm not the kind of person/leader who would open this kind of difficult conversation or take this kind of risky action." Notice the voice that says these things, become aware that the hesitation is nothing more than a reinforced learned reaction. Of course you can take the action, have the conversation! It may not be pretty, but it's doable.

This week pay attention to your thoughts and to where your inner voice points you. What are the thoughts you have? Where is your attention drawn? What patterns of behavior or thinking seem to be ever present? When nodding off to sleep at the end of the day consciously and purposely define the attitude of mind you wish to engage in the morning. Otherwise, you'll fall off to sleep unconsciously reinforcing a composite attitude of mind that is made up of all feelings and reactions of the day. Journal your insights daily...not with an intent to judge or change them. Simply journal to become more aware. Remember, energy follows attention. Where is your energy being unconsciously focused? This simple act of becoming more aware will begin the process of revealing different choices that will allow you to become more effective at leading – both your organization and your life.

"Your mind will take the shape of what you frequently hold in thought, for the human spirit is colored by such impressions. You could leave life right now (*memento mori*). Let that determine what you do and say and think."

~ Marcus Aurelius, *Meditations*

The one "super power" humans possess that sets us apart from the rest of the animal kingdom is our imagination. Developing our imagination as a leadership tool rather than what most experience as simply day dreaming is a powerful way to manifest what you want and desire in life.

Development of this sort requires discipline and practice. Your imagination is capable of incredible insight and force. Use it to feel, see, and fully experience reality the way you want it to be. Marcus Aurelius says in this week's passage that "...the human spirit is colored by such impressions." It's in this sense that we experience imagination existing at the threshold of our spirit. And, our spirit continuously seeks to be expressed in ever greater ways.

It's not a coincidence that leaders such as Walt Disney and Thomas Edison have been quoted as saying, to paraphrase, "If you can dream it, you can be and do it."

This week take time daily to vividly imagine your future exactly like you wish it to be. Create a vision board and journal about it. Experience yourself thinking, speaking, behaving and feeling as if it was manifest now. Imagine people interacting with you in ways that are consistent with your vision. Your mindset will begin to take the shape of that which you frequently hold in thought!

"It is only by a change of consciousness, by actually changing your concept of yourself that you can 'build more stately mansions'...It is of vital importance to understand clearly just what consciousness is. The reason lies in the fact that consciousness in the one and only reality, it is the first and only cause-substance of the phenomena of life. Nothing has existence for man save through the consciousness he has of it."

~ Neville Goddard, *The Power of Awareness*

Bucket lists...

I wrote my first bucket list when I was 18 years old and just graduating from high school. I had 20 things on that list ranging from travel the world to flying an airplane. I grew up on a farm in rural Oregon and was the only one of my siblings to go to university. We certainly weren't wealthy and I didn't personally know (or even know of) people that had done most of the things on my list. At that time my sense of my "identity" (my self consciousness) in no way included having, doing or being any of these things. They just seemed to me to be worth experiencing. I kept revisiting that list and, interestingly, I found that within 10 years *every* item on that first bucket list had come to pass. Looking back on that time I didn't exert any undo effort to make these things real. As a matter of fact, you might say I simply "followed my nose". Opportunities seemed to appear out of nowhere and one unplanned "yes" or carefully considered "no" (more on this in a later week) positioned me in ways I couldn't have deliberately planned. The key to this was keeping my consciousness in the game and, over time, my sense of identity – my concept of myself – had transformed. I also realized I needed to start dreaming/imagining "bigger"!

Goddard continues in *The Power of Awareness* to say that "I can only give what I AM, I have no other gift to give. If I want the world to be perfect, and who does not, I have failed only because I did not know that I could never see it perfect until I myself become perfect. ...all outward appearances are but states of mind externalized."

"I regard consciousness as fundamental. I regard matter as derivative from consciousness. We cannot get behind consciousness. Everything that we talk about, everything that we regard as existing, postulates consciousness."

~ Max Planck, Nobel Prize-winning physicist
and the father of quantum theory

Quantum theory literally and completely upended our understanding of reality. So much so that physicists today are still grappling with the implications. Made obsolete were Newtonian cause/effect models of the universe that could be applied to all of reality. Our observable world came to be understood in terms of the "observer phenomenon" in which the simple act of "observing" a quantum event changed it. In this world view there is no "effect" or "cause" without the participation of an observer. Indeed, today there is gathering evidence that there may be *no* objective reality and that two "observers" can view the same event with completely different cause/effect correlations. This is the crux of Planck's observation. This is important for us as leaders because we live in a quantum reality. Everything we observe and experience at a macro level with our senses is rooted in a quantum field of interactions. The "observer" – our consciousness – is behind everything we experience as real.

This week entertain the notion that this might be true. Behave "as if" the act of observing makes a difference. Not observing with your objective senses however – use your imagination. That difficult person you have to deal with? Rather than wanting them to change, change how you "observe" them in your mind. Imagine them being their best version of themselves and then act, feel, think and speak in alignment with *that* reality.

"I want to talk to you about the livingness there is in being yourself. It has at least the merit of simplicity, for it must surely be easier to be oneself than to be something or somebody else. Yet that is what so many are constantly trying to do; the self that is their own is not good enough for them, and so they are always trying to go one better than what God has made them, with endless strain and struggle as the consequence. Of course, they are right to put before them an ideal infinitely grander than anything they have yet attained – the only possible way of progress is by following an ideal that is always a stage ahead of us – but the mistake is in not seeing that its attainment is a matter of growth, and that growth must be the expansion of something that already exists in us, and therefore implies our being what we are and where we are as its starting point. This growth is a continuous process, and we cannot do next month's growth without first doing this month's; but we are always wanting to jump into some ideal of the future, not seeing that we can reach it only by steadily going on from where we are now."

~ Thomas Troward, *The Hidden Power*

Because we are charged as leaders to inspire ourselves, others and our organizations to continuously grow and expand it's natural to look around for role models and examples from those who have succeeded. In doing so comparison is a good place to start. However, it's a very poor place to stay. Many people will attempt to copy the characteristics and style of those they think of as being successful. In doing so they risk losing themselves. We want to be cautious when adopting and adapting what we think is the successful behavior of others.

A useful metaphor is to imagine having suits of clothes available for different occasions. You'll put on your gym wear if you're planning on exercising and your formal wear when attending a fancy gala. But are you "comfortable" in your attire? Do you wear the suit or does the suit wear you? If the suit is wearing you it's likely due to the fact that your consciousness – your sense of self – isn't congruent with the suit. It isn't fitted well and you feel awkward and out of place wearing it. To the observer you appear inauthentic.

Authenticity is core to a leader's effectiveness. But how do you define authenticity if continual growth implies continual change? Explore and journal about this question this week.

MONTH 2

AWARENESS

~ NOTICING ~

> "Let all your efforts be directed to something, let it keep that end in view. It's not activity that disturbs people, but false conceptions of things that drive them mad."
>
> ~ Seneca, *On Tranquility of Mind*

Energy will follow your attention. Said another way, it's your attention not your intention that drives the actions you take. A conflict between attention and intention causes confusion and will drive you and others crazy.

This week notice what you notice. Pay attention to where your focus is drawn. Pay attention to what grabs your attention. Notice when your energy shifts. What came into your awareness just prior to that shift? Our behavior is consistent with the meaning we make up about what we're noticing. Is "it" threatening or beneficial?

Most people operate unconsciously in their lives...they are on auto pilot. Much of what triggers our actions has become so habituated that it is out of our conscious awareness. Recent studies indicate that by the time a person reaches the age of 30 up to 95% of their behavior is unconsciously triggered. This is what we mean by mindset.

The value in becoming increasingly aware of where your attention is draw is that you can become increasingly responsive rather than reactive. Over time, you begin to transform your mindset. You have more choice because you can begin to consciously assign meaning to what your noticing. And because your meaning making drives your behavior you will likely begin to develop different behaviors thereby producing different results.

"Some things are in our control, while others are not. We control our opinion, choice, desire, aversion, and, in a word, everything of our own doing. We don't control our body, property, reputation, position, and, in a word, everything not of our own doing. Even more, the things in our control are by nature free, unhindered, and unobstructed, while those not in our control are weak, slavish, can be hindered, and are not our own."

~ Epictetus, *Enchiridion*

One of the foundational tenets of Stoic philosophy is that there will always be things out of our control and that the *only* things I can control are my thoughts, actions, feelings. As a leader it's absolutely crucial to take this to heart. Railing against what we can't control is at best a waste of energy and at worst incredibly destructive. And, to pile on just a bit you might also consider that the one thing we definitely can't control is the outcome from any of our behaviors.

The internalization of this Stoic "truth" – that we can control our behaviors but not their outcomes, let alone the outcome of other people's behaviors, leads one to a calm acceptance of whatever happens knowing that we have done our best given the circumstances.

As a leadership example of this consider Admiral James Stockdale. In 1965 on September 9th (my birthday) he was shot down over North Vietnam during the Vietnam War and spent seven and a half years as a prisoner of war in what was derisively called the Hanoi Hilton. As he was parachuting to a landing near a small village he whispered to himself: "Five years down there at least. I'm leaving the world of technology and entering the world of Epictetus." For the next 7 ½ years he endured torture multiple times, solitary confinement for years at a time and through it all maintained a sense of equanimity. He internalized Epictetus advice to play whatever part Fate had allotted to him to the best of his abilities and kept in mind that he would lose only if he succumbed to two things – loss of self-respect and fear. Fear could only be possible if he thought he had control over the outcomes of his behavior *and* he knew the only thing he did have control over was his behavior.

When we notice that we are becoming attached to what we think the outcome should be we lose our ground of being and our resourcefulness. We become reactive rather than responsive. Being non-attached doesn't mean we don't care. Celebration and disappointment are both appropriate responses to outcomes *and* the true point of focus needs to be "did I do all I could, where I was, with what I had?" This week have this be your focus.

> "We envisioned a new kind of business culture – a culture that puts people first and where true success is measured *by the way we touch the lives of people.* I'm completely obsessed with creating a culture in which all team members can realize their gifts, share those gifts, and go home each day fulfilled."
>
> ~ Bob Chapman, CEO Barry-Wehmiller

Barry-Wehmiller is a US$2.1 Billion company. Bob Chapman's passion for "noticing" where the organization's and its employee's attention is focused has made all the difference in how the company performs and, specifically, in how it has managed to keep its employees passionately engaged. The company is a manufacturing behemoth that has intentionally acquired a portfolio of "broken" companies and turned them around with the simple ethos highlighted in this week's quote. Most leaders will say that their people are their greatest asset. But when push comes to shove this is seldom the case. In Bob Chapman's case it is his north star. For me, Chapman's leadership philosophy can be summed up in this manner: "We make a difference not just a product."

This week notice how you and your organization are making a difference. What is the quality of that difference? How do people – your employees, customers, suppliers and community – feel about themselves when they are in the presence of your product or service? How do they feel about themselves when they are in *your* presence? We are constantly touching the lives of others. It can't be avoided. The challenge is to be intentional about this rather than having it just happen as a consequence of being asleep.

"All profound things, and emotions of things are preceded and attended by silence...silence is the general consecration of the universe."

~ Herman Melville, Philosopher and Author

In today's extraordinarily noisy world grabbing a moment to simply be still can be difficult. Add to this societal (and business) expectations that seeming "idleness" is to be avoided...after all "idle hands are the devil's workshop."

Research shows that the average person experiences approximately sixty to seventy thousand thoughts a day. And, most of these are typically the same thoughts day after day and most of these are also "negative" in nature to some degree. Thoughts like "I'm not good enough", "what if it goes wrong", "nobody will buy in to this", "that's too risky", "I can't afford that", and so on. How do we navigate through such a minefield to find the jewels that will move us and others to greater success? Cultivating stillness of mind dials down the noise to the point where what I call soul can actually be heard. The philosopher and psychiatrist Carl Jung, to paraphrase, said of the soul that it is the part of anything that gives voice to being more, wanting more, striving for more. We want to be able to hear that voice because it's core to who we are and what we can become. Too

often that voice is so faintly noticed as to be functionally absent from our
experience of life, living and growing.

This week practice listening for that voice. If you have a mindfulness practice pay attention. If you don't have one I can't recommend strongly enough that you begin one. It can be as simple as sitting quietly for five minutes without external distractions and focusing your attention on your breath. As a leader "all profound things…are preceded and attended by silence."

Month 3

Awareness

~ Flow ~

"Life is a series of natural and spontaneous changes. Don't resist them – that only creates sorrow. Let reality be reality. Let things flow naturally forward in whatever way they like."

~ Lao Tzu, *Tao Te Ching*

The experience of being in flow is nature and life's way of signaling that we are connected. Connected to life and connected to what matters to us. The flow state is effortless, which isn't to say that there is no effort involved. Rather, it seemingly just unfolds...right place, right time, right actions with the right people being in precisely the right positions. This happens when I leave who I think of as myself behind and just show up with a "now" focus that moves me out of being aware of space or time. Another way of saying this is that we enter a flow state when we become fully present. By way of illustration recall a great movie you've seen or a book that was impossible to put down. When watching the movie or reading the book you likely became so engrossed in what was unfolding that you literally were not aware of time's passage or of anyone else around you. You were "in" the book or the movie...it flowed.

Another useful metaphor is that of a river flowing to the ocean. There is a main current in this river and if you're in it not much effort is required to keep you moving. However, if you move away from this main current it becomes more difficult to maintain both speed and direction. You have to paddle harder, eddies appear that pull you out of the river's flow and you may even end up stranded in still water.

Where is the current in your life? It's typically close to your purpose in life. When you connect with it life flows and successes seem to come with ease. When we become distracted thinking things should be different than they are or we listen to someone else's admonition to "be" different we perturb this current. We move out of flow.

This week pay attention to where and when a sense of ease seems to be present with what you are doing. Notice any patterns associated with this. What is being fulfilled? What "for the sake of" is being attended to?

"Your principles can't be extinguished unless you snuff out the thoughts that feed them, for it's continually in your power to reignite new ones...It's possible to start living again! See things anew as you once did – that's how to restart life."

~ Marcus Aurelius, *Meditations*

You will get out of flow. Life will become difficult. Work will seem like a burden. Your marriage will have difficulty. Your kids will be difficult. You will have money problems. The challenge is to not to look at any of these things as being indicative of what you will have or experience tomorrow.

The great trap almost everyone falls into is using one's senses to determine what is real and what is possible. We look at our bank account to decide what's possible. We succumb to the feeling of helplessness and/or hopelessness when things go sideways. We hear things that cause us to question our dreams. It's important to remember that what we are sensing is *only* real beyond that moment if we allow the thoughts to continue.

The role of our imagination is to keep us moving toward our ideals – seeing and sensing possibilities beyond our senses. Developing this capability is crucial to living and leading a life that is ideal. As the Mad Hatter said to Alice in *Through the*

Looking Glass, "Sometimes I've believed in as many as six impossible things before breakfast."

This week practice Marcus Aurelius' call to action. "See things anew as you once did..."

"I'm not in the White House. Tried for that job. I
didn't get it. So, all I can do from where I am is to
say, 'All right, how do we get things done from
here?'"

~ Mitt Romney, US Senator and
2016 Republican Presidential Candidate

One of the quickest and surest ways to interrupt flow is to be at
odds with what is. Thinking that things should be different than
they are suggests we have control of things we don't have control
over. All we ever have control of are our thoughts and behaviors.
The outcomes linked to our actions are out of our control. This is
one of the basic tenets of stoic philosophy.

The mark of true leadership – whether it be organizational or
personal – is the ability to hold the big picture and not be
attached to results. I can't control where or how the river is
flowing. I can control how I think and move in and on that river
as my domain. Learning to master my thinking and my attitude
is key. This is the true power of awareness.

Any increase in awareness is *automatically* accompanied by an
increase in the numbers and kinds of choices I have available.
Part of developing personal mastery is noting which choices are
in service of my purpose and which are in service of egoic
desires. As Senator Romney points out, we want to become

capable of regularly asking a considered question of "...how do we get things done from here?" This is what moves us back into flow and it is what will keep us in flow more consistently.

This week pay attention to not being solely informed by what your five senses are telling you is real and possible. Leadership is the art of revealing possibilities. Practice being an artist by bringing your awareness and your attention to your intuition, your reasoning and your imagination.

"To enter into the spirit of anything, then, is to make yourself one in thought with the creative principle that is at the center of it...look at life as the one thing that is, whether in you or around you; try to realize the livingness of it, and then seek to enter into the Spirit of it by affirming it to be the whole of what you are."

~ Thomas Troward, Philosopher,
Entering Into The Spirit Of It,
The Collected Essays of Thomas Troward

In this particular essay philosopher Thomas Troward explores flow from the perspective of one's *relationship* with that which one aspires to be, do, or have. As long as what I seek is experienced as being outside of me I am vulnerable to moving out of a flow state. It's Troward's position that everything has a spirit that informs its existence and if I am able to literally *enter into the spirit* of it I begin to match its expression and any activity involved in its manifestation becomes effortless. My work is experienced as being in flow with the essence, the spirit, of my desire.

Think of it this way...when I enter into the spirit of a book, the spirit of a movie or the spirit of a game I stop worrying about what I'm doing. I simply let it unfold. The outcome will be what it will be. I'm connected to the spirit that informs the game, the book or the movie and not the outcome. The focus of my relationship has shifted.

My "job" is to show up and give all that I can give in the moment. I cease judging what's going on around me. I respond to external (and internal) perturbations thoughtfully rather than react to them reflexively. This allows me to maintain a sense of equanimity rather than being off balance. I'm fully engaged and I'm secure in the knowledge that all I can ever do is to do my best. The experience of fully doing my best moment to moment is the experience of flow. It's the embodiment of how Earl Nightingale defines success as being "...the progressive realization of a worthy ideal."

This week get lost in what you're doing in the same way you would get lost in a great book, an amazing movie or a fascinating conversation...by "entering into the spirit of it."

PART 2

The DOMAIN

of

CONTEXT

MONTH 4

CONTEXT

~ MEANING ~

"Don't aim at success—the more you aim at it and make it a target, the more you are going to miss it. For success, like happiness, cannot be pursued; *it must ensue*, and it only does so as the unintended side effect of one's personal dedication to a cause greater than oneself or as the by-product of one's surrender to a person other than oneself. *Happiness must happen, and the same holds for success: you have to let it happen by not caring about it. I want you to listen to what your conscience commands you to do and go on to carry it out to the best of your knowledge. Then you will live to see that in the long-run—in the long-run, I say! – success will follow you precisely because you had forgotten to think about it.*"

~ Viktor Frankl, *Man's Search for Meaning*

Almost everyone misunderstands the purpose of a goal. Most people think it's about getting or achieving something we haven't yet gotten or achieved. As Frankl mentions in the above quote the realization of a goal is often the "unintended side effect". The true purpose of a goal is to grow...as an individual and as an organization. Goals must inspire if they are to be of utility and inspiration only occurs when I'm stepping outside of my comfort zone. In order to do so the goal – any goal – needs to be *meaningful.*

Meaning is personal. I can't tell another why a goal would be meaningful to them. I have to invite an inquiry..."if we were to realize this goal what would it make possible for you that you wouldn't get to have, do or be?" This is followed by "is that worthwhile for you?" These simple questions (which are almost never asked of people) are an invitation to step outside of what is known, to step outside of what is comfortable, and to step into something that has seemingly been beyond reach.

Meaning. Without it we are left with boredom. Without it there is no desire. Without it we (and our organizations) simply go through the motions, doing just enough to get by. With it the focus shifts. It moves me away from the humdrum of routine. It provides a reason beyond my paycheck to come to work. It spurs innovation and creativity. It is the foundation of high levels of emotional engagement.

This week ask questions designed to discover meaning when discussing your and your organization's goals. Find a way to discover the embedded "for the sake of what?" that makes the goal meaningful.

"What man actually needs is not a tensionless state but rather the striving and struggling for some goal worthy of him. What he needs is not the discharge of tension at any cost, but the call of a potential meaning waiting to be fulfilled by him."

~ Viktor Frankl, *Man's Search for Meaning*

The late leadership guru Warren Bennis wrote many books (over 30) and articles about leadership. One of my favorites was a co-authored article (with Robert Thomas) that appeared in the September 2002 edition of the Harvard Business Review. It was entitled *Crucible of Leadership.* In the article the authors describe a number of leaders that experienced incredibly daunting challenges ranging from labor disputes, 16 years of solitary imprisonment in Communist China, sexism and racial/religious bigotry and the calamitous impact of unexpected change and death. Each of these experiences represented what Bennis and Thomas referred to as a crucible. A crucible is a trial or test that creates points of deep self-reflection that forces me to question who I am and what really matters. They test our patience, belief systems and core values.

In the article the authors state that "We believe that great leaders possess four essential skills, and, we were surprised to learn, these happen to be the same skills that allow a person to find meaning in what could be a debilitating experience. First is the ability to engage others in shared meaning...Second is a distinctive and compelling voice...Third is a sense of integrity (including a strong set of values)...But by far the most critical skill of the four is what we call 'adaptive capacity.' This is, in essence, applied creativity – an almost magical ability to transcend adversity, with all its attendant stresses, and to emerge stronger than before. It's composed of two primary qualities: the ability to grasp context, and hardiness...It is the combination of hardiness and the ability to grasp context that, above all, allows a person to not only survive an ordeal, but to learn from it, and to emerge stronger, more engaged, and more committed than ever."

How well developed is your "adaptive capacity"? There will always be tension and pressure as you strive to manifest bolder and larger dreams. Owning the *meaning* of the dream, striving to the see the bigger picture (context) and being able to persevere in the face of adversity are ways we bring possibility into reality.

This week continue to take some time to reflect on the meaning clarifying question "For the sake of what?" as you engage in the various activities that make up your week. Having a clear and consistent answer to this question is one key way that we develop our "adaptive capacity."

Epictetus tells the story of Agrippinus, who refused to not rock the boat during Nero's reign and who refused to conform or moderate his independent thinking. Why do this, Agrippinus was asked, why not be like the rest of us? *"Because you consider yourself to be only one thread of those which are in the tunic. Well then it was fitting for you to take care how you should be like the rest of men, just as the thread has no design to be anything superior to the other threads. But I wish to be purple, that small part which is bright, and makes all the rest appear graceful and beautiful. Why then do you tell me to make myself like the many? And if I do, how shall I still be purple?"*

~ Epictetus, *Enchiridion*

Meaning informs all of our behaviors and is fundamentally linked to our values. This is one of the main reasons that, as a leader, you need to know yourself well. What are your core values? How do they guide and inform your behavior? How do they help keep you centered when in the midst of uncertainty and turbulence?

A key question all leaders eventually face is "how do I know what to do when I don't know what to do?" Without the clarity provided by well understood and integrated values it's far too easy to go along just to get along and in the process lose yourself and any claim to the uniqueness that helps you and your mission stand out.

This week again continue to practice asking the meaning clarifying question "for the sake of what?" each time you feel the urge to compromise who you are and what you're up to. Notice how important that question is.

Sometimes you will go along with the crowd. But when you have considered this question prior to doing so at least you will be mindfully aware of the potential upsides and downsides of doing so. Your actions will then have meaning that is relevant to you and what your wanting to manifest. Insuring that meaning stays on your radar is the way you keep your core values intact.

> "Always remember that to argue, and win, is to
> break down the reality of the person you are
> arguing against. It is painful to lose your reality, so
> be kind, even if you are right."

> ~ Haruki Murakami, *Colorless Tsukuru Tazaki*

What does it mean to be "right"? The dictionary defines the word in a number of ways. As an adjective it means morally good, justified, or acceptable (e.g., that was the *right* action to take). As a noun it's defined as that which is morally correct, just, or honorable (e.g., he had every *right* to be angry). Unfortunately, neither of these definitions actually answers the question of meaning.

A *meaningful* definition of "right" is: "any action or any thing that behaves or is present in a manner that is consistent with my beliefs." This is an operational/functional definition of the word and it is one that leaders need to pay particular attention to. Everyone wants to be right...I have never met anyone that likes the experience of being wrong. Even though I can rationalize the experience by looking for the lesson in the experience the *feeling* associated with being wrong is something almost everyone prefers to avoid. Being wrong violates my sense of how reality *should* be constructed, it violates my values and what I value and, most importantly, it will always create resistance. The need to be and to feel right is one of the most powerful drivers you will encounter in a relationship. It's so powerful in fact that most people would rather be right than get what they say that they want. As a simple example of this imagine a recent disagreement you had with your significant other. It's likely that what you say you want is a loving, nurturing and respectful relationship with this person. Now review that disagreement in light of this want. Chances are *very* high that continuing to argue for the rightness of your position compromised your ability to achieve that want. This happen all the time.

Far too often the focus is on being right. We end up arguing to "win" versus to understand. The challenge for leaders is to remain focused on what they want. In so doing, the need to be right about how something is done, about how someone should behave or think, about preferences of any kind will begin to be less dominant. This shift in focus is a very powerful way to continuously connect with and vet what you say are your most sacred values. It is also a way to keep others connected to you and your outcomes. Co-creating coordinated movement is an exercise in manifesting a shared and valued reality. It is the opposite of invalidating another's reality.

This week become aware of how strongly the need to be right informs your thinking and behavior. What's more important...being right or having what you say you want?

MONTH 5

CONTEXT

~ INVITATION ~

"There are not more than five musical notes, yet the combinations of these five give rise to more melodies than can ever be heard. There are not more than five primary colors, yet in combination they produce more hues than can ever be seen. There are not more than five cardinal tastes, yet combinations of them yield more flavors than can ever be tasted."

~ Sun Tzu, *The Art of War*

Co-creating coordinated movement is an art. When you think of art you must also think of the artist. As a leader, a truly effective leader, you are an artist working with incredibly complex materials – people. How you invite them to participate in your creation and how you score, conduct and blend their interactions takes skill. Anyone can break an egg into a skillet. To bake a world class soufflé requires skill and mastery. It requires attention as well as intention. Some of the finest dishes I've eaten or sunsets I've observed were comprised of surprising ingredients that came together in totally unexpected ways.

As a leader you want to be willing to experiment with blending and leveraging your people in unexpected ways to assist you in getting where you intend to go. This is what is meant by "co-creating coordinated movement." As Jim Collins says in his bestselling book **Good to Great**, "... *leaders of companies that go from good to great start not with 'where' but with 'who.'*

They start by getting the right people on the bus, the wrong people off the bus, and the right people in the right seats. And they stick with that discipline – first the people, then the direction – no matter how dire the circumstances."

Any organization is simply an assembly of people in relationship. In relationship obviously with each other. But they are also in relationship with anything and everything the organization is comprised of...values, work processes, goals, vision, equipment, vendors, tools, etc. Everything we encounter in our workplaces has a relational dynamic associated with it. What is the relationship people have with your objectives? How do you invite these varied relationships into a co-created collaboration?

This week pay attention to the richness of the diversity you have to work with. How are you blending them? How are you designing their interactions? As a chef would, consider what's too much and what's too little.

"When I see an anxious person, I ask myself, what do they want? For if a person wasn't wanting something outside of their own control, why would they be stricken by anxiety?"

~ Epictetus, *Discourses*

Equanimity is a state of psychological stability and composure which is undisturbed by experience of or exposure to emotions, pain, or other phenomena that may cause others to lose the balance of their mind. How do you invite this into your experience of life and leadership? And, perhaps more importantly as a leader, why would you want to do so?

We are fields of energy that others interact with – our moods are contagious. When our energetic field is perturbed and in turmoil those around us feel it and make meaning up about it.

Consequently, as leaders, we want to be able to manage our mood states. The most effective way I have ever found to do this is simply to recognize what is and what isn't in my control. What is in my control are my thoughts, my feelings, my emotions and my behaviors. Everything else is out of my control. Anxiety is the consequence of wanting something outside of our control. We get worked up, excited, nervous and focused on the short term.

This type of thinking and approach to leadership and living is a muscle that needs to be exercised in order to become fully useful.

Equanimity is the evidence that I am succeeding in developing this muscle. The world around us – society, the news, pop culture, world and local events – all conspire to tell us we should be "in charge" of everything if we are to be effective as leaders. When I "invite" equanimity into my life I have acknowledged and owned my true source of power which is simply that over which I actually have control. The Stoic Philosophers called this our *prohairesis*. It's a reasoned choice to not be at effect of what goes on around me. It's the kind of cultivated choice that allows us to withstand *with equanimity* the inevitable pressures, problems and even hostile attacks from others that come from being a visible and audacious leader.

This week pay attention and strive to not be at effect of what your five senses tell you is "real". What's real is what you have in your control – your thoughts, feelings, attitude, and behavior.

"Ultimately, man should not ask what the meaning of his life is, but rather must recognize that it is he who is asked. In a word, each man is questioned by life; and he can only answer to life by answering for his own life; to life he can only respond by being responsible."

~ Viktor Frankl, *Man's Search for Meaning*

Meaning doesn't just appear. It must be invited. It must be discovered and nurtured. This process is a great example of the power of both awareness and context. We begin to notice where and with what do we resonate. What values, what behaviors, what ideals light us up? In what environments and situations do we shine? In that noticing we have access to choices that weren't noticed before and thus begins the process (if we're disciplined and principled) of integration that begins to forge our sense of a meaningful life. In Frankl's words, we can "...only answer to life by answering for his own life; to life he can only respond by being responsible."

As a leader this process of invitation into meaning is seldom wielded well. Rather, the default is often a process of telling others why something should be meaningful. In this version the meaning is not the other's, it's meaning that's relevant only to the leader. This type of "invitation" is typically framed in the language of importance (e.g., I need you to do this because it's important for "x" reason). While the importance is very likely valid it's crucial to keep in mind that the context of importance does not create the same level of commitment or engagement as the context of meaning. Co-creation implies shared meaning. You and I can probably coordinate our movement around a declaration of importance but coordinated movement is only half of the leadership definition. Co-creation is critical to shared ownership and it's rooted in shared meaning.

This week practice *inviting* others to let you know from their perspective why and how your request is meaningful to them. Explore with them what the successful fulfillment of your request makes possible for them that wouldn't otherwise occur. In what ways are those possible outcomes meaningful to them?

"Thus, in scientific research, a great deal of our thinking is in terms of theories. The word 'theory' derives from the Greek '*theoria*', which has the same root as 'theatre', in a word meaning 'to view' or 'to make a spectacle'. Thus, it might be said that a theory is primarily a form of insight, i.e. a way of looking at the world, and not a form of knowledge of how the world is."

~ David Bohm, *Wholeness and the Implicit Order*

David Bohm has been described as one of the most significant and influential theoretical physicists of the 20th century who contributed unorthodox ideas to quantum theory, linguistic ontology, neuropsychology, and the philosophy of mind. The above quote was summarized by him in a far more popular way when he said *"The ability to perceive or think differently is more important than the knowledge gained."*

When you think of perspective as simply another way of describing context you begin to understand its power. When we shift our perspective we quite literally invite alternative realities to appear. Our willingness to suspend attachment to a preferred point of view is fundamental to moving beyond conflict (which is *always* rooted in separate parties being attached to differing points of view). As Bohm's quote suggests shifting perspective will, in the long run, serve to improve our effectiveness in co-creating coordinated movement.

Leadership causes movement. Conflict tends to stop or slow movement. When you begin to ask questions oriented toward understanding another's point of view you invite participation and engagement. Such questions don't invite yes or no as responses...they invite dialogue. Dialogue is literally an exploration of ideas (theories). The word itself is comprised of two Latin derivatives – *dia* (around) and *logos* (ideas). Such an exploration can often lead to a reassessment of what I thought was "true". It can cause me and others to "think differently." As a leader your primary concern will ideally always be to the continuation of movement toward a desired ideal. Inviting shifts in perspectives is one of the most effective ways to achieve this. To quote Bohm one final time, *"What prevents theoretical insights from going beyond existing limitations and changing to meet new facts is just the belief that theories give true knowledge of reality (which implies, of course, that they need never change)."*

This week notice what assumptions are supporting the conclusions that we call our point of view. Explore their validity and not the validity of the point of view itself.

Here's to developing your "shifting perspective" muscle!

PART 3

The DOMAIN

of

COMMUNICATION MASTERY

MONTH 6

COMMUNICATION MASTERY

~ CLARITY ~

CLARITY MEANS CLEARNESS.
CLEAN WATER RUNNING DOWN
A MOUNTAIN HAS CLARITY. SO
DOES A LOVELY SINGING VOICE:
IT'S CLEAR AND PURE.

IF YOU BRING CLARITY TO A
SITUATION, YOU HELP PEOPLE
SEE WHAT REALLY HAPPENED
BY CLEARING UP
MISUNDERSTANDINGS OR
GIVING EXPLANATIONS.

"From Rusticus...I learned to read carefully and not be satisfied with a rough understanding of the whole, and not to agree too quickly with those who have a lot to say about something."

~ Marcus Aurelius, *Meditations*

How do you study? If you're like many people your study habits were developed and organized around successfully passing tests. You memorized facts so that they could be recalled when it came time to sit for your exams. This strategy is obviously useful if all you want to do is pass an "test" in order to move onto the next challenge or level. It's a process of accumulating information and knowledge. However, it's not a process that foster true learning, which is the integration and transformation of that knowledge into meaningful and useful behaviors and thinking.

I, like many of my friends, have a home library. Mine contains an eclectic and interesting (at least to me) collection of books touching on a variety of topics such as physics, cosmology, linguistics, ontology, philosophy, mind, psychology, business, and leadership. I've read most, if not all of them cover to cover. However, I would say I only truly "know" a very small handful. These are the books I've studied. These are the books that contain knowledge I want integrated into my way of being and thinking. A couple of the books I've read continuously for years.

There are selected passages and chapters I've read and re-read, that I've studied and meditated on over and over. Notes fill (and overflow) the margins of the pages in many cases. I've digested the sentences, attempted to put the author's words into my own "language" and intentionally looked to my life for examples that would illustrate what the authors are wanting to bring to light and life.

Why do such a thing? The simple answer is I want to be as effective at leading and living my life as I possibly can. I'm also lazy. I have little desire to reinvent the wheel when I don't have to! Wisdom is distinctly separate from knowledge in that it is *applied* knowledge. Knowing when and how to apply knowledge requires its integration into who I am. It allows for clarity of action when all around me seems muddied and uncertain. It allows me to answer the question, "How do I know what to do when I don't know what to do?" This is called "Learning Agility." Korn/Ferry International conducted research assessing nearly one million executives worldwide on leadership effectiveness and their research shows that Learning Agility is a reliable indicator of leadership potential because learning agile people "excel at absorbing information from their experience and then extrapolating from those to navigate unfamiliar situations."

This week study, study, study. You'll find it leads to greater clarity when you are facing great uncertainty.

"It goes back to a conversation I had with NBA star Vince Carter when I was consulting with them. He said at 38 the behaviors for him to keep playing were clearly defined. It "took what it took" and he had to decide whether to do them or not...That conversation helped me better explain the simple truths behind success to athletes. It also safely allows for people to choose an average set of behaviors, but the outcome will be pre-determined."

~ Trevor Moawad, *It Takes What It Takes*

Moawad is a renowned mental conditioning expert who works with some of the most elite athletes in the world. In his book *It Takes What It Takes* he covers extensively the kind of work that needs to be done in order to achieve our biggest goals. In essence, it comes down to just what the title suggests...doing what it takes.

The beauty of this kind of clarity is the simple choice it presents. The work you put in, the traits you develop, shapes the kind of person and leader you become as well as the results you ultimately produce. This is true of the individual as well as the organization. There is a simple axiom I often use in my coaching work with leaders..."people will give you what they perceive you're willing to settle for. They will never give you what you ask for."

In terms of Communication Mastery this axiom is worth its weight in gold. It's not what you say…it's how you "be" as you say what you say. The leader is always setting the ceiling on both expectations and performance. They do this by setting and consistently demonstrating a congruent example. High standards are communicated by doing what it takes. Moawad says, "Behavior, which you've drilled into your muscle memory will dictate what happens next."

Clarity, discipline and desire are the tools that keep you moving. What does it take? This week identify to the best of your ability exactly what needs to be done and how you need to approach the job. Commit to it because you will be challenged and distracted. And, be sure that there is a compelling "for the sake of what" that keeps the flames of your desire burning.

"Vision is about asking the big questions: Where are we going? Why are we going there? How will each of our stakeholders be in a better place when we get there? A good vision sets goals, inspires all team members, and allows leaders to make decisions that move us toward where we are going."

~ Bob Chapman, CEO Barry-Wehmiller
Everybody Matters: The Extraordinary Power of Caring for Your People Like Family

Of course, vision matters. That being said, vision is one of the most poorly understood and poorly utilized "tools" in the leadership toolbox. In the early part of my consulting career I literally stumbled across a rather generic article on vision. While I don't recall much from the article there was a sentence that has always stayed with me: "It's not important what a vision is. What's important is what a vision makes possible."

Your ability to communicate clearly about future possibilities is absolutely key to moving the possibility into probability in people's minds *and bodies so* that it can be transformed into reality via co-created coordinated movement.

This ability was literally embodied by the late Steve Jobs and was described as being his "reality distortion field." This "field" was a way of communicating a possibility with energy, excitement, detail, feeling and present tense description that left the listener with the experience of believing that it was not only possible but also in disbelief that it wasn't already so. A "good" vision, as mentioned by Bob Chapman, is one in which separation between present and future has been eliminated. The "vision" exists now...we just haven't arrived yet!

This week move through your conversations – with others and with yourself – as an *embodiment* of the possibility, the vision, that you wish to manifest. Feel as if it is real, speak as if it is real, behave as if it is real, write and think as if it is real. Distort reality!

"It is quite impossible to unite happiness with a yearning for what we don't have. Happiness has all that it wants, and resembling the well-fed, there shouldn't be hunger or thirst."

~ Epictetus, *Discourses*

In order to reconcile what is with what we desire as a result it's necessary fully be clear about the fact that everything that ever was or ever will be has already been created. It's *simply* now a process of manifesting what is desired. This is not magical thinking. This is how the Universe actually works. And, I italicized simply because it can seem anything but simple. Your energetic positioning impacts and affects your ability to co-create coordinated movement. If you are dissatisfied, discouraged and coming from a mindset of scarcity you're communicating that something is missing, that something is amiss. Nothing is ever truly missing. And, as long as you continue to take action in service to your desired result nothing is ever amiss. This is just what it looks like as the process of manifestation unfolds.

Equanimity is the outward expression of an inner state of happiness and stillness. The word is defined as "...mental calmness, composure, and evenness of temper, especially in a difficult situation." This is what you want to attend to exhibiting.

Co-creating coordinated movement is all but impossible when you and others run around with hair on fire because something seems amiss.

Be clear, it's already here – it just hasn't manifested yet – and then communicate from that place of clarity. Insist that you and others behave, think, feel, and speak as if this were so and you will experience what you desire as your reality.

Month 7

COMMUNICATION MASTERY

~ COMMON MEANING ~

"Communication is simply the ways people use to work out common meaning with one another."

~ Virginia Satir, *Family Psychologist*

I've spent the vast majority of my career in non-English speaking countries working with and consulting to companies that used English as their working language although it was not native to most of their employees. As you might imagine with such scenarios, communication difficulties often arose. These took the form of issues as simple as time zone confusions and as complex and potentially enterprise threatening as total misalignment on mission critical objectives. These problems were present not because people weren't bright enough to know to take care when communicating. The problems were present because people didn't truly understand that meaning drives everything. In the rush to get things done assumptions were made and, as the old saying goes, when you make an assumption you make an "ass" out of "U" and "me".

Here is a seemingly straightforward math problem to illustrate what I'm referring to: $3 + 3 \times 3 + 3 = ?$. The possible answers are:

a) 21

b) 36

c) 15

While we all have a basic understanding of math, this simple arithmetic problem causes a great deal of argument because people will process the equation in a way that is meaningful to them because explicit meaning that leads to deciding the correct processing sequence of the numbers isn't explicitly provided...it's left to individual interpretation. Is it a simple linear process (i.e., 3+3=6; 6x3=18; 18+3=21)? Or should the multiplication be done first (i.e., 3x3=9 giving the sum of 3+9+3=15)? Or is the correct answer 3+3=6 x 3+3=6; 6x6=36)

Language – spoken and written – is symbolic. Whether the language is math, English or Swahili the words we use are symbolic placeholders that are used to confer meaning *and* those symbols often are interpreted in different ways.

In order to co-create coordinated movement you and they need to have the same meaning underpinning all that you do. The vast majority of disagreement and conflict can be traced back to simple misunderstandings of meaning.

This week, when you encounter a difficulty stop and pause. What different meanings are in play?

"If someone is able to show me that what I think or do is not right, I will happily change, for I seek the truth, by which no one was ever truly harmed. It is the person who continues in his self-deception and ignorance who is harmed."

~ Marcus Aurelius, *Meditations*

Most people would rather be right than get what they say they want. Think about that sentence for a moment. How often has it played out in your life and in your interactions with others? The functional definition of the word "right" is anything or anybody that behaves in a manner that is consistent with my beliefs. The meaning in my and your behaviors, thinking and feeling is almost always filtered through the lens of "right". This feels right; this is the right action to take; these are the right thoughts to pursue. Being "right' is for most the primary determinate of meaning.

I have never met anyone who likes the experience of being wrong. Avoiding the experience of feeling wrong drives much of the behavior and thinking that we find in organizations and in life. This is one of the major reasons that co-creating coordinated movement is so difficult. Successfully achieving that kind of movement requires people to be vulnerably aware of what meaning is informing their decisions.

We've all had silly arguments about something as trivial and inconsequential as who squeezed the toothpaste tube in the "wrong" place. I have a preference about what is the "right" way to squeeze the tube. My wife has no such preference. And, if you're paying attention in those times you may have noticed a small internal voice asking, "What are you doing? You said you wanted a loving, respectful marriage and you're arguing about this!?" If you're like me, when I've noticed that voice my rejoinder is to tell it to shut up because "I'm winning!" I'm being right at the expense of what I've said I wanted because it's more meaningful to "win" the argument in that moment. We need to keep in mind what the BIG win is.

Co-creating coordinated movement requires common meaning. It isn't about being right. It's about discovering different and valid perspectives that morph (hopefully) into a common meaning that allows us to move forward with greater elegance. We do this by being willing to suspend attachment to my preferred point of view long enough to truly evaluate another's.

This week when encountering differences pay particular attention to feeling the need to be right and notice the subtle and not so subtle ways you're making the other wrong.

"Between stimulus and response there is a space. In that space is our power to choose our response. In our response lies our growth and our freedom."

~ Viktor Frankl, *Man's Search for Meaning*

There is a very distinct and powerful difference between a thoughtful response to something and an emotional and reflexive reaction. Rather than jumping to conclusions about what you think something meant, take a pause to reflect. This ability to pause is a cornerstone of emotional intelligence which research indicates comprises up to 90% of a leader's overall effectiveness.

As you pause notice what you're feeling...angry, jealous, frustrated, sad, happy. Pay particular attention to the bodily sensations that comprise that feeling...hot, cold, tight, tense, shallow breath, rapid heartrate, sweaty palms. Then, take a moment and inquire within. What *specifically* triggered the sensation? What meaning did you assign to the trigger? Is it true? Is it true now? How do I know? How could I find out? What *response* would be most appropriate in order to facilitate co-creating coordinated movement. Remember, the future is nothing more than the consequence of now's decisions.

This practice of pausing before engaging takes no more than 5-10 seconds. The clean-up required for a misinformed reaction can take days. Your choice.

"Your brand is what people say about you when you're in the room."

> "Your brand is what people say about you when
> you're not in the room."
> ~ Jeff Bezos, *CEO of Amazon*

People tell stories. As a matter of fact, meaning is created and communicated *solely* through the use of stories. Customers judge companies primarily upon how they perform relative to their promise...the same is true for how leaders are judged. Stories are involved in both judgements – a story about the promise and its meaning and a story about the performance and its meaning.

Stories are personal and they directly impact your ability to co-create coordinated movement. As a data point consider that, according to Gallup research, customer loyalty plummets an average of 29% if customers don't have a strong belief in the company's ability and commitment to keep its promises.

As a leader you are a brand and your brand is a story steeped in the meaning people have made up about who you are, what's important to you, and what you're up to. What's important to keep in mind is that your story will always get in the room before you do. Why this is important is because of Bartlett's First Law of Leadership: "People will give you what they perceive you are willing to settle for...they will never give you what you ask for."

This Law requires you to be very clear about what your *nonnegotiables* are. These are the behaviors, the levels of performance, the exhibitions of values that are your red lines. When you are engaged in co-creating coordinated movement it's crucial that you are totally clear – with yourself and others – about the promise you are making.

This week take out a piece of paper and make a list of all of the things your followers will *always* receive from you as a leader. These are nonnegotiable. Fail to deliver and the story of you becomes squishy. Consistently deliver and you're in charge of creating a story that will serve you.

Month 8

COMMUNICATION MASTERY

~ INFLUENCE ~

"Opinions are the cheapest commodities on earth. Everyone has a flock of opinions ready to be wished upon anyone who will accept them. If you are influenced by "opinions" when you reach decisions, you will not succeed in any undertaking."

~ Napoleon Hill, *Think and Grow Rich*

You are a literal, virtual, walking talking symbol of the result you wish to achieve. The energy that is your thinking, your feelings and your emotional state has influential impact. Simply said, you influence others most directly by your "state of being" and not by the words you use. The question, "How do others feel about themselves when they are in your presence?" is fundamental to the art of influence because behaviors are always proceeded by feelings.

Napoleon Hill summarized in his seminal book that one of the key traits exhibited by all of the successful people he interviewed while writing the book was the quick making and subsequent adherence to a decision. These folks – Carnegie, Ford, Edison, Firestone – all were able *and willing* to not be swayed by opinions once they had decided. Unless and until convincing factual evidence (not opinion) could be provided they stayed the course.

When you consider this trait of making and sticking to a decision within the context of Bartlett's First Law of Leadership – "People will give you what they perceive you'll settle for…" – you begin to appreciate just how powerfully influential a decision can be.

This week notice what you settle for when faced with push back. The argument against what you want may seem reasonable *and* reasonable people tend to get reasonable results. Reasonable people are swayed from their decisions by reasonably existing circumstances and opinions. Because it is all about possibility leadership is often an unreasonable activity.

"Leadership is not about a title or a designation. It's about impact, influence and inspiration. Impact involves getting results, influence is about spreading the passion you have for your work, and you have to inspire teammates and customer."

~ Robin S. Sharma, *Author*
The Monk Who Sold His Ferrari

Pay particular attention to the three attributes of leadership that Sharma identifies – impact, influence, and inspiration. All three are so tightly linked that they are essentially indistinguishable from each other and when mindfully woven together they create the fabric of the whole that we call influence. Essentially, they are the levers of influential communication.

Impact refers to not only the visible and felt consequences of your actions. It's also, and more fundamentally, the consequence of your presence – how you show up – as a leader. Leaders cause movement. It's a cause/effect correlation and the catalyst for the initial cause of any movement you're causing is the other's perception of you. Your metric for the quality of that movement needs to be effectiveness. Is the action an example of co-created coordinated movement? Is it elegant or is there a significant amount of "clean-up" that needs to be done? What can help you calibrate your impact is a simple question..."what's too much and what's too little?"

Influence in the context of Sharma's quote specifically refers to the emotional content of your message. I invite you to consider his definition of influence as only a portion of the much larger context of meaning. A simple observation about how information is generally processed by individuals is "how I describe something determines how I feel about it which, in turn, influences my behavior." The description process is the meaning generating process and your emotional energy (passion) conveys FAR more meaning than the words you use to get your message across. Ideally, you want to have others resonating emotionally with the passion you feel for your vision.

Which leads us to **inspiration**. The philosopher Carl Jung has been quoted as saying "Without this playing with fantasy, no creative work has ever yet come to birth. The debt we owe to the play of the imagination is incalculable...All the works of man have their origin in creative fantasy."

Imagination lives at the threshold of spirit. It's the gateway to the soul and the soul is our source of inspiration. When we are inspired our soul is awakened to possibility. And possibility is what is too often missing in many organizations. Possibility to be more, to do and have more. Not an incremental more. A more that calls on us to transcend what we know and to transform who we are. That sort of "fantasy" inspires. This was Steve Jobs great secret.

This week invite others to play with the fantasy that is your and their future. Invite them to explore questions like "what if...?" Take the constraints off and imagine what a future could be that isn't hemmed in by what others would think or what resources seem to be in short supply. Notice how inspiring this is when you begin to feel it as being a possibility.

"Think twice before you speak, because your words and influence will plant the seed of either success or failure in the mind of another."

~ Napoleon Hill, *Think and Grow Rich*

The phrase "our people are our greatest asset" has been bandied about for decades but very seldom do people in organizations feel valued. Interestingly, when you think of the meaning assigned to various words the meaning typically attached to the word asset from an accounting perspective involves depreciation over time for tax purposes. It's not an accident that most people in most organizations feel depreciated. Employees are accounted for on the P&L and Balance Sheet as an *expense*. As a consequence, if you see your employees as an expense they become an aspect of your business that you seek to minimize – and that shows up in your words, your thinking, your energy, and your actions.

The opposite of this all too typical approach is worth considering. If you truly consider your people to be assets you will see them as vital to your business and you'll seek to amplify their impact and make them more valuable. You'll begin to look for ways to cultivate and enhance them so that they can become more productive and thereby more profitable for your business. This isn't altruistic...it is good business. How to do this is an exercise in monitoring your thinking and interactions.

Researchers writing in a Harvard Business Review article ("How to Play to Your Strengths", January 2005) made the point that "It is a paradox of human psychology that while people remember criticism, they respond to praise. The former makes them defensive and therefore unlikely to change, while the latter produces confidence and the desire to perform better."

This week pay attention to whether you view your people as a cost to your business to be minimized or as an asset to be uplifted and improved. Then "think twice before you speak."

"Is my intention good? That is the initial question, for the intention determines the nature of the essence in everything. What is the most beautiful form in which I can express the good I intend? That is the ultimate question; for the true Beauty which our work expresses is the measure of the Power, Intelligence, Love – in a word, of the quantity and quality of our own life which we have put into it. True Beauty, mind you – that which is beautiful because it most perfectly expresses the original idea, not a mere ornamentation occupying our thoughts as a thing apart from the use intended."

~ Thomas Troward, *Beauty,*
The Collected Essays of Thomas Troward

Consider Troward's quote and assume for a moment that the question "Is my intention good?" is the foundational leadership question. How would this question influence how you approach what you do and how you are as a leader?

The difference between influence and manipulation is one of intention. Co-creating coordinated movement (leadership) is a mutually beneficial activity. If your intention is that only you benefit others will feel manipulated. Make no mistake about this. The mechanics and tactics that are utilized by leaders to cause movement in and with others are exactly the same whether they are manipulating or influencing...it's your intention that makes the difference.

This is where the notion of "beauty" comes in. Beauty, as Troward (and Plato) describe it, is the outward manifestation of an inner spirit or enlivening force. It's what is experienced when you are influenced by a beautiful sunset, a beautiful song, or the beautiful work of a master craftsman. The "author" and you as the recipient both benefit.

Beauty is the metric by which the elegance of your influence can be measured. Thinking of beauty in this way, "Is your work elegant?" provides you with the parameters you need to assess your influence. Elegance refers to the lack of a need to clean up after your done. No unintended consequences. The spirit of your intent was good and it invited others to participate fully with you. That's influence.

This week think and act in terms of beauty. Begin with Troward's question "Is my intention good?" Then consider "What is the most beautiful form in which I can express the good I intend?"

PART 4

The DOMAIN

of

COMMITMENT

Month 9

COMMITMENT

~ I AM ~

"I am not all contained between my hat and my boots."
~ Walt Whitman, *American Poet, Song of Myself*

Who I am is nothing I can observe. My thoughts, my feelings, my behaviors are all things I can observe. My results, the activities of others, the economy are also things I can observe. By definition, if I can observe something I am not it. Therefore, who am I? This is more than a philosophical question. This question has great import in terms of how you carry yourself as a leader.

What is being expressed *as you?* When we discuss and explore the nature of commitment the default for most people is to think of being committed *to* something out there...a goal, and ideal, a result, an outcome, a relationship. The language you'll typically hear spoken for this declaration is, "I am committed to...." Note where the object of the commitment is oriented. Outside of self. It's out there in the future somewhere. I can metaphorically point to it and, because I can point to it, I am not it. And because I am not it I can't truly own it.

As a leader you are first and foremost a symbol of the result you espouse. Everything you do, say and emotionally express is filtered through the lens of commitment by those you're interacting with. Do they experience you *being* – do you experience yourself *being* – that which you say you're committed to having?

Rather than being committed to..., you want to **become** a commitment. The language you use for this is, "I AM a commitment to..." This is a declaration, an embodied ownership, that becomes the standard others coordinate around. It is not separate from you...it *is* you.

This week practice internalizing and becoming a commitment of that which you desire. I am a commitment! Practice feeling, walking, talking, thinking, breathing, dreaming as if this was your identity. This is your **I AM**. Be mindful of anything you place after those two words.

"When you know that consciousness is the one and only reality...you are free from the tyranny of second causes, free from the belief that there are causes outside of your own mind that can affect your life...If man's concept of himself were different, everything in his world would be different. His concept of himself being what it is, everything in his world must be as it is. Thus, it is abundantly clear that there is only one I AM and you are that I AM. And while I AM is infinite, you, by your concept of yourself, are displaying only a limited aspect of the infinite I AM.

~ Neville Goddard, *The Power of Awareness*

This passage will undoubtedly challenge some belief systems (part of what comprises our personal mindset). That being said, if you were to assume that this passage were true what are the implications for how you lead others, yourself, and your organization? What "second causes" have you been letting control the way you lead your organization and life? What might you do differently if you embraced the notion of consciousness being the "one and only reality"? Another way of thinking about this is that there is nothing (an no one) out there except yourself.

We are, each of us, the center of our own universe. Everything that we encounter emanates from us. Everything we experience through our senses is assigned meaning by us. Nothing is "meaningful" in its own right. This process of assigning interpreted meaning is so automatic and imbedded in our mindset that, unless we're paying attention, we seldom notice it. As such, we want to become intimately familiar with who we are beyond our mindset because the "I Am" that we are is infinitely resourceful and when understood and appreciated is an incredibly powerful and stable foundation from which to lead our lives.

The leadership question "How do I know what to do when I don't know what to do?" is a crucial question because, as you and your organization grows, you will invariably find yourself in unfamiliar territory. This is when your answer to who "I Am" comes into play. If you've done your work and developed a sense of this you have the foundation you need in order to navigate uncertainty. At this point allowing the emergence of knowing what to do when you don't know what to do will become second nature.

This week revisit your sense of the infinite "I Am". Remember that what will limit us in life is not who we think we are, it's who we think we are not.

"The soul is like a bowl of water, and our impressions are like the ray of light falling upon the water. When the water is troubled, it appears that the light itself is moved too, but it isn't. So, when a person loses their composure it isn't their skills and virtues that are troubled, but the spirit in which they exist, and when that spirit calms down so do those things."

~Epictetus, *Discourses*

I once lived in Japan for a number of years. While there I began to study the martial art of Aikido. As with other similar martial art traditions, as my training progressed and I became more proficient it was time to move up a level which would be signified by a different colored belt to wear with my training ghee. In order to do so a proficiency test needed to be passed. Part of the test involved what is known as a rondori – a practice whereby the other students form a circle around the one being tested and come at him/her. Successfully meeting the multiple challenges simultaneously coming at them is evidence of proficiency and level mastery.

My sensei (teacher) was a 72 year old wisp of a man who was a true master of the art. Watching him in a rondori I was awe struck at the ballet of movement he exhibited. He was unflappable, gracefully elegant, and seemingly centered the entire time. I commented on this to him and asked how long had it taken him to develop the ability to be totally centered the entire time. He smiled and said he wasn't. He said he knew where his center was and could quickly come back to it when he was knocked off balance.

Life will continuously knock us off balance. Knowing who I Am is my center. Developing the familiarity necessary to quickly come back to this center is key to my resourcefulness as a leader. It provides the proverbial port in a storm from which I can set sail anew. When we are knocked off balance the natural untrained tendency is to overcorrect in search of coming back into balance. Being centered is where we are most resourceful. Being centered allows for an omnidirectional response to external stimuli. When we are off balance our concern is safety and our compensatory move is almost always reactionary.

I Am a commitment. Having this as part of your sense of identity provides the necessary center when circumstances around you are in upheaval. This week think of yourself in the middle of a rondori solidly centered as your commitment and elegantly handling all that is coming at you.

> "The more tranquil a man becomes, the greater is his success, his influence, his power for good. Calmness of mind is one of the beautiful jewels of wisdom."
>
> ~ James Allen, *As A Man Thinketh*

Commitment is an interesting word in terms of the behaviors that it invites. Some people are averse to committing because they imagine that by committing they are limiting their freedom in some way. This is why many will hedge their bets so to speak and try to conditionally commit. "I'll do this if and/or when that is done." This is not commitment. This is an indication that their sense of self, their I Am, is not comfortable identifying with the commitment.

Commitment is like pregnancy. You can't be sort of pregnant. It's all or nothing. You either are or you aren't. This is why we use the language "I Am a commitment." It removes all doubt as to whether you're fully in! As long as commitment is allowed to be conditional (an oxymoron by the way) the mind will be perturbed and confused and a confused mind does not act.

Calmness, as highlighted in the above quote by James Allen, is a consequence of knowing who I Am so that any commitment I make is aligned with this identity. There is no question, there is no equivocation, there is certainty. I will do this because I Am this. And because I Am this I can't not deliver on the commitment. External circumstances don't perturb or sway me. Doubt is not part of my thinking. And, this calmness of mind influences all around me. They experience me *being* the commitment and align their behaviors with me accordingly. You are now positioned to co-create coordinated movement.

This week notice the way external conditions attempt to compromise your willingness to commit. Then recall Neville's quote that "When you know that consciousness is the one and only reality...you are free from the tyranny of second causes, free from the belief that there are causes outside of your own mind that can affect your life." Then come back to the center of I Am.

COMMITMENT

~ PERSONAL MASTERY ~

"Ask yourself the following first thing in the
morning: What am I lacking in attaining freedom
from passion? What for tranquility? What am I? A
mere body, estate-holder, or reputation? None of
these things. What, then? A rational being. What
then is demanded of me? Meditate on your actions.
How did I steer away from serenity? What did I do
that was unfriendly, unsocial, or uncaring? What
did I fail to do in all these things?"

~ Epictetus, *Discourses*

The point of this quotation from the Stoic Philosopher Epictetus
is two-fold: 1)reflection is valuable and, 2)a reflective ritual is not
only valuable it's a requirement to your effectiveness. Let's look
at this a bit closer.

Reflection is how you keep yourself on course as a leader. During
the course of your day you'll get some things right and some
things wrong. Some of what you do will work and some won't
work. Reflection allows you the space to identify if there are
themes beginning to take root. Themes include such things as the
need to be right, the need to be in control, the need to dominate,
the need to have the answer, the need to look good. Themes can
also include patterns of self-doubt or second guessing that show
up around certain events, people or situations. The key here is
that you're looking for themes, for ways in which thinking,
feeling and behaving are sneakily becoming habitual and out of

your day to day awareness. Notice the patterns and you can interrupt them. The idea is to take some time to look inward and examine. Taking time is what the Stoic Philosophers advocated more than almost anything else and it is this practice around which Self Mastery is organized.

Rituals are the secret to many leader's success. Rituals can take many forms...you can meditate, exercise, write, walk in nature, read for the sake of study, breathe, or journal about your thoughts, fears and feelings regularly. The point isn't what you do it's that you do. There is an old saying that "practice makes perfect." This isn't necessarily true. What is true however is that "practice makes habits!" When developing habits that lead to Self Mastery rituals are your best friend. They don't have to be cumbersome or numerous. Again, the idea is to have time to reflect and center yourself and this is what rituals make possible.

This week identify what ritual you have that start or end your day. If none are apparent, what ritual could you develop that will provide a small keystone to your building greater Self Mastery?

"You cannot know if you will be successful or not. You can only prepare for battle and it must be done with all of your heart and with all of your consciousness. In that manner, you will have an edge."

~ Sun Tzu, *The Art of War*

Self Mastery does not a guarantee a specific outcome. However, without it you as a leader will almost certainly fail in the long run. Leadership is an inside out process. And when put in the context of co-creating coordinated movement the beginning is learning to masterfully co-create coordinated movement with yourself.

Self Mastery is a discipline requiring honest reflection, a willingness to challenge closely held beliefs, a desire to grow and to be more, commitment to a generative ritual, and the courage to be vulnerable. As a discipline it's important to recognize that this is not a one and done process. Self Mastery is perhaps the most challenging and most rewarding journey you will ever undertake.

I have spent a fair amount of time in Africa amongst members of the Masai tribe. I've been made an elder in the tribe and have come to appreciate the age old rites of passage that signify transition from one stage of life to another. Each of these rites involve degrees of Self Mastery. As an example, when boys move from puberty to junior warrior status one of the rituals involves a circumcision ceremony performed without the use of anesthetic. The initiate is expected to have mastered his emotional and physical self to the point that he can undergo such a surgery without any indication of discomfort. The preparation involved to reach this level of mastery is significant and it is intended to inform the warriors entire approach to life going forward. As Sun Tzu indicates in the above quote, "You can only prepare for battle and it must be done with all of your heart and with all of your consciousness."

As a leader your Self Mastery is your secret weapon. It gives you an edge in that it provides the intellectual, physical, emotional and spiritual rigor necessary to meet any challenge. While there is never a guarantee of success, being as prepared as possible is what you can dedicate your life to.

This week reflect on what area of your various lives (intellectual, physical, emotional, spiritual) could be further developed. Pick only one and devise a developmental plan for yourself in this area. Small steps. Simple steps. Steps that will enable you be become more masterful in and with that area of life.

> "The spirit, the will to win, and the will to excel are the things that endure. These qualities are so much more important than the events that occur."
>
> ~ Vincent Lombardi, *NFL Hall of Fame Coach*

Lombardi was the legendary coach of the world champion Green Bay Packers NFL football team. Arguably the greatest football coach of all time (sorry Bill Belichik), he's on the short list of history's greatest coaches, regardless of sport. His ability to teach, motivate and inspire players helped turn the Green Bay Packers into the most dominating NFL team in the 1960s. Over the course of his career with the team, he led them to a 98-30-4 record and five championships, including three straight titles. The team never suffered a losing season under the Hall of Fame coach.

Lombardi's winning methodology as a coach was surprisingly simple...insist on being the best at all times. He firmly believed that you can only become a leader after developing your character. He was once quoted as saying, "Perfection is not attainable, but if we chase perfection we can achieve excellence." He embodied Bartlett's First Law of Leadership...People will give you what they perceive you're willing to settle for, they will never give you what you ask for.

Settling was not in Lombardi's vocabulary. Many, especially some of his players, thought his expectations of them were often times unreasonable. Lombardi however knew that unreasonable people tended to achieve unreasonable results. Tellingly, he applied the same standards to himself. He knew that a leader can't build a team, department or company that's much different than who they are. His focus on Self Mastery, on discipline, on being honest with himself, on setting ever higher standards began with himself as a coach and as a person. Again, he once said that "I'm no better nor less than the next man. But the thing about me is that I always knew what my acts would mean. I was lucky...I found singleness of purpose early on." Self Mastery is rooted in clarity of purpose...for the sake of what am I doing and living?

This week take time, in the words of Ralph Waldo Emerson, to ask, "What is my job on this planet? What is it that needs doing that I know something about, that probably won't happen unless I take responsibility for it?"

"The true self of each person is the mind. Know therefore that you are a god. For a god is someone who moves, who feels, who remembers, who looks to the future, who rules over and guides and directs the body he is master of, just as that Supreme God directs the universe. And just as this eternal God controls the universe, which is partly mortal, so too your eternal spirit directs your fragile body."

~ Cicero, *Scipio's Dream*

When speaking about Self Mastery what we're really speaking about is the mind. While no one knows where the mind actually is we all possess one. It's perhaps the most powerful tool we have access to and, like any tool, in the hands of a master it is capable of crafting works of incredible beauty.

When Cicero speaks of each of us as gods he's not being heretical. He's acknowledging that the spirit that informs who each of us is and, ultimately, what each of us does with our lives is in our hands. Our job as a leader – of life and of people – is to develop mastery over the use of this amazing tool. All of the ancient text and sages knew this. It's part of the perennial philosophy.

Each of us in our lives will be whipsawed by external circumstances of which we have little or no control. But our mind? We have absolute control over this amazing tool. From Cicero's perspective it gives us god-like powers to manifest new realities, to dream wild possibilities and then shepherd them into reality. We truly are the center of our universe and, with mastery, we can control that universe the way the Greek gods on Olympus did.

The philosopher Neville Goddard said, "To realize your desire an action must start in your imagination, apart from the evidence of the senses, involving movement of self and implying fulfillment of your desire." Master the use of your imagination.

This week take time to dream. What's possible? If there were absolutely no constraints what would be your ideal life? Your ideal company? Your ideal relationship? Don't just imagine...add feeling and emotion into the picture. Act this week as if the possibility were a reality.

PART 5

The DOMAIN

of

TRUST

TRUST

~ ALIGNMENT ~

"Trust is the glue of life. It's the most essential ingredient in effective communication. It's the foundational principle that holds all relationships."

~ Stephen Covey, *The Seven Habits of Highly Successful People*

We all know and appreciate the importance of trust in our lives. Without it, as a leader you're doomed. With it you can work miracles. So, here's the question for you to consider this week...what is it? How do you know when it's present and how do you know when it's missing?

When talking about trust we are often using the word as a placeholder for something specific that is not explicitly identified. "She's not trustworthy" may or may not be a true statement but we can't really know until and unless what's being referenced by the word trust is specifically known. The problem definitely can't be fixed unless this is known. How do you "fix" broken trust if you don't know what's missing?

Trust is complicated. What I look for in a relationship that leads me to believe I can trust or not is going to be different than what you are looking for. For example, competence may be my main criteria for assessing whether I can trust you or not. If I have the experience that you're competent I'll trust, if I think you're not competent I won't. For you caring may be the key criteria. If you feel I care about your well-being you'll trust and if you feel I don't you won't. We have differing criteria for what we think is necessary for trust to be present and these criteria are typically not explicitly know by ourselves and are almost never known by others.

Co-creating coordinated movement requires trust. It is probably the single most important ingredient. Knowing what trust is enables you and your partner(s) to get things back into alignment when something happens to knock it out. You have to be specific about what's needing to be addressed. Simply saying "trust is broken" doesn't provide you or them with the information required to repair it.

This week notice trust – its presence or its absence – in the relationships you have...especially the ones that are most crucial to your success. Pay particular attention to how you know. What specifically do you need to have present in order to trust. Is it competence, character, caring, consistency, courage, or something different. It's typically not one thing but if you're paying attention you'll notice that there is a dominant attribute that you sort for.

"In this age, I don't care how tactically or
operationally brilliant you are: if you cannot create
harmony - even vicious harmony - on the
battlefield based on trust across service lines,
across coalition and national lines, and across
civilian/military lines, you need to go home,
because your leadership is obsolete."

~Gen. Jim Mattis, *U.S. Secretary of Defense*

Harmony...it's the consequence of co-created coordinated
movement. It's what "elegant" feels and looks like in that there
are little to no unintended consequences to your actions that
require you to expend unplanned time and resources cleaning up
after yourself. Harmony, "even vicious harmony" is a sign that all
parties are on the same page and are aligned in their
commitment to producing the desired outcome. Another way of
saying this is that all parties *trust* that what they are engaged in
is built with the foundational integrity of buy in.

General Mattis' reference above to "vicious harmony" may seem
like an oxymoron but it is truly an acknowledgement of how
healthy conflict is resolved in high performing organizations and
teams. Conflict is a necessary element in any and all
relationships and how it is addressed is crucial. Is the conflict
about the issue or is it about the personalities? This is the
difference between warranted and unwarranted conflict. Leaders

that are focused on co-creating coordinated movement attend to insuring that the trust necessary to enter strong conversations that help define exactly what is being addressed is present. When trust of this sort has been developed the tendency to go along in order to get along disappears. You want, indeed need, to get strongly held points of view on the table *for the sake of* having a fully vetted outcome as the objective. Alignment occurs when people *feel* they have been heard. It doesn't necessarily occur when agreement has been reached.

This week pay attention to your and your peoples' willingness to truly hear what the other is saying. This will require vulnerability and vulnerability is rooted in trust. Trust that you can handle what evolves in the dialogue…you may end up changing your mind.

> "Great companies that build an enduring brand
> have an emotional relationship with customers that
> has no barrier. And that emotional relationship is
> built on the most important characteristic, which is
> trust. "
>
> ~Howard Schultz, *Founder, Starbucks*

Your brand promise is something that your customers, your suppliers, your vendors and your employees need to be able to count on. When you pay attention to the most enduring and successful companies you will notice that they almost never compete in the marketplace solely on price or quality. Their focus is never organized around satisfaction...the focus is on building and sustaining loyalty.

This isn't to say that satisfaction isn't important. It is. But it's also a purely transactional metric. A single satisfying transaction doesn't translate to loyalty. However, a single dissatisfying transaction may well translate to "I'll never shop here again." You need to build a relationship that honors the feelings and needs of all parties and that is deep enough to accommodate the inevitable dissatisfying transaction. And, make no mistake, this is easy to say...hard to do.

Co-creating coordinated movement isn't just something that involves your employees. This is a process that involves *all* stakeholders that are touched and impacted by what you and your organization are doing...and, what you are promising to do.

During a recent trip overseas involving a Mediterranean cruise my baggage was "lost". Not overnight but for 10 days! I got them back two days before the end of the cruise which necessitated purchasing enough clothes to get me through the trip. The airline (British Air) was horrible in addressing my needs. They were impossible to contact for updates and the compensation process was slow and very complex. On the return trip my bags were once again lost! This time by a different carrier. Again, they didn't reappear for almost two weeks. This carrier (Alaska Airlines) was wonderful. They were easy to access for status updates, handled my need for, once again, new clothes (I was leaving the next day on a business trip to Asia) and their personnel were consistently considerate as I vented my frustration. I *felt* valued by Alaska. I felt as if I was an imposition with British Air. I trusted that Alaska would follow through on their promise. I did not trust British Air to deliver.

Alaska Air has my business and I will inconvenience myself in order to fly with them. Will your customers do the same with you? That's the power of trust!

This week do a "trust audit" of your relationships. What can you do to improve? The ball is in your court to do this.

"To have faith is to trust yourself to the water.
When you swim you don't grab hold of the water,
because if you do you will sink and drown. Instead
you relax, and float."
~ Alan Watts, *Philosopher*

Where is your center? I earlier mentioned my Aikido sensei and his comment about being able to quickly return to center as being the key to his mastery of Aikido. His trust in himself to know this center allowed him to be able to handle the adversity life inevitably confronted him with. It allowed him to align all of his internal resources in order to move elegantly through his life. He relaxed and floated.

The great paradox about trust is that it's never about anything or anybody external. It's always about myself. The more familiar I am with what comprises my center the more confident and trusting I become.

As a leader there will be times (many of them) when you feel lost and don't know what to do. As Alan Watts says, "To have faith is to trust yourself to the water." The water is your center and developing the capacity – the faith – to trust that it will support you when all appears lost is the way the question "how do you know what to do when you don't know what to do?" is answered.

Developing a practice that keeps you attuned to this center and that allows you to develop your familiarity with it needs to be one of your first leadership objectives. It's fundamental to your success because trust is fundamental to successful relationships.

This week go silent. Look within and note where and what your strengths are. Take out a piece of paper and make a list. How do you exhibit them? How do you access them? Recall times when each of them has come into play and served you well. When did you over extend their use? If they were controlled by a rheostat rather than an on/off switch how would you dial them forward and backward.

Become intimately familiar with these strengths. The more familiar you are with them the safer and more confident you'll feel. This in turn will lead to you behaving more freely. You'll step out more, you'll take more risks, you'll stretch and grow. You'll let yourself become uncomfortable because you know you can handle what comes at you. And, even if you stumble you'll know how to start over.

Month 12

TRUST

~ CONFLICT ~

"On great teams - the kind where people trust each other, engage in open conflict, and then commit to decisions - team members have the courage and confidence to confront one another when they see something that isn't serving the team."

~Patrick Lencioni, *The Five Dysfunctions of a Team*

The relationship between courage and trust is often overlooked. Yet the very concept of trust is rooted in risk. That there are no guarantees in life should be obvious to most yet it's amazing how many want certainty before they are willing to commit.

Trust requires vulnerability and before I'm willing to be vulnerable I have to know and have confidence that I can handle the consequences. This is the paradox inherent in trust. We think it's about the other or the circumstances but what we're really trusting, what we're really risking, is our ability to deal with what being vulnerable may entail. What would they think of me, what if I'm wrong, will they question my competence or sincerity if I raise the issue? Will I put my job at risk?

Leaders that are creating environments where co-creating coordinated movement is the expectation do so with an eye to ensuring people feel safe enough to give voice to their concerns. Not only does the desired outcome or goal have to be meaningful. So too does the expectations for what kind of behavior is acceptable. Going along to get along will not work. False harmony is a poor second for true alignment.

This week consider these questions: What kind of behavioral ground rules have you set in place for your team? How well skilled are the team members in making sure that the disagreements are focused on the right things and don't devolve into personal attacks? How do you build into the organization's culture the sense (and expectation) that being "right" is less important that getting what you and your team says is important? Most importantly, how are you modeling this?

"When team members trust each other and know that everyone is capable of admitting when they're wrong, then conflict becomes nothing more than the pursuit of truth or the best possible answer."

~Patrick Lencioni, *The Five Dysfunctions of a Team*

In his book *The Five Dysfunctions of a Team*, Lencioni describes a very elegant model for understanding how teams will typically go off the rails.

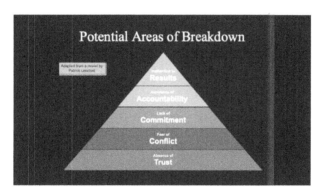

When you look at this model you'll note that everything rests on the foundation of trust. The pursuit of truth and/or the best possible answer is what you're after. What gets you there is trust.

Co-created coordinated movement is evidenced in the results that are produced. When trust is present conflicting points of view can be explored and understood. When this occurs people fully understand what specifically they are committing to produce. When that clarity is present so too is clarity about who specifically is accountable for what (teams aren't accountable, individuals are). With clearly understood and agreed to accountability standards your and your team's ability to produce result will seldom be in doubt. And, when things begin to go sideways (and they will), blame will seldom be an issue. You simply can come back to where in the framework the breakdown occurred and begin to rectify it.

The questions you will use as a leader to make this possible are "What's working?" and "What's not working?". You don't use questions oriented around what was or is right/wrong or good/bad. And, you keep the conversation factual...what's the evidence. "This didn't work and specifically here is what and where and how it didn't work."

Trust is built on the experience of safety. This is why you want to know yourself well. You develop the confidence to be vulnerable by knowing who you are...what's your foundation? Then, you create an environment where others feel safe to fully show up.

"Did I offer peace today? Did I bring a smile to someone's face? Did I say words of healing? Did I let go of my anger and resentment? Did I forgive? Did I love? These are the real questions. I must trust that the little bit of love that I sow now will bear many fruits, here in this world and the life to come."

~ Henri Nouwen, *Dutch Theologian*

Tina Turner sang "What's love got to do with it?". Simply, everything.

I'm not talking about romantic love. I'm referring to the love that is present as a consequence of realizing that literally everything is connected. Another word for this is compassion. In times of conflict it's easy to dismiss and forget this universal connection. In times of conflict it's common to experience emotions other than compassion. Anger, frustration, defensiveness and righteousness are only some of what we and others likely experience is such times. When we're involved in a conflict situation with another it's common to want to be right and to be in control. These are two of the surest ways to ensure that ill-will and resentment will be part of any resolution.

We, each of us, have views of the world and what we call reality that differ from everyone else's. We have arrived at a conclusion about what is going on and so have they. It's useful to remember that *all* conflicts are conflicts of competing conclusions. There will *always* be differences. Doing what you can to minimize the likelihood of these differences becoming the focus rather than the mutually desired outcome, is why, as a leader, you want to be able to approach any situation with the thought of leaving the other with the experience of uplift.

Do they *feel* validated and understood or do they feel wrong and judged? This is not the same as you agreeing with them. It's simply the acknowledgment that their view of reality is valid *from their current point of view.* This a loving think to do. It values their world view without sacrificing yours. And, it fosters the development of trust in the sense that they experience they are held in regard and not being made wrong by you. As the late Zig Ziglar once said, "If people like you, they'll listen to you, but if they trust you, they'll do business with you."

Using inclusive language (words like and, we, us, our) will go a long way to reinforcing that your intent is co-creation. Make no mistake, disagreements occur. Of that there is no question.

This week be sure to keep a modicum of love present – for yourself and for them – it's how you maintain connection.

"I judge you unfortunate because you have never lived through misfortune. You have passed through life without an opponent—no one can ever know what you are capable of, not even you."

~ Seneca, *On Providence*

We end the year's practices with this quote from Seneca, who I consider to be one of the most influential of the ancient Stoic philosophers.

Conflict and trust go hand in hand. We have no control over what life dishes up for us. Storms happen, markets shift, people die and new people come into our lives...relationships change in unexpected ways. The measure of who we are as a leader is one of tempering. It's the unexpected that throws us off balance that is the invitation to discover what within us we can trust. Without the conflict presented by the unexpected (what we call misfortune) we can't truly know what we are capable of.

A review of my life to date reveals events that, at the time, felt calamitous. Looked at today the death of my wife, the loss of a major client, the market collapsing, a divorce, the untimely death of my brother, being fired from a job I loved were all crucibles that provided me with the opportunity to excel. In the face of each of these events I grew. I discovered more of me that I could count on.

At the end of the day conflict and trust do go hand in hand. Having developed the awareness of who you are, what your strengths are and what your center is made of, you are equipped to trust that you will know what to do when you don't know what to do. You'll have the courage to move and to act knowing that you'll get it wrong sometimes. But also knowing that you will land on your feet. As Sun Tzu said in *The Art of War*, "The successful person has unusual skill at dealing with conflict and ensuring the best outcome for all."

An old mentor of mine suggested something that, this week, you can practice with when things don't go as planned. "It is what it is. Harvest the good. Forgive all the rest."

LEADERSHIP MINDSET MASTERMIND

As I mentioned in the introduction to this book there is nothing on this planet that is not touched in some way by the activity of leadership. By investing a year of your time and life on these weekly lessons your leadership competency has improved and the difference you make as you have learned more about co-created coordinated movement has been significantly enhanced.

Your Leadership Mindset is either going to inhibit or enable your leadership effectiveness. This year long journey was specifically designed to invite you to examine what comprises your Leadership Mindset. Hopefully, you've made some discoveries and some adjustments. Your development as a leader is a life long journey. I have learned to draw on the knowledge of mentors, philosophers, coaches, and other business leaders as part of my journey. You can find some of these lessons as well as many more resources to help support you on this journey – readings, articles, programs, videos, focused coaching – by going to www.blainebartlett.com.

One unique and powerful resource that you can tap into is a dedicated and focused LEADERSHIP MINDSET MASTERMIND. This Mastermind is a 52-week facilitated deep dive into the lessons and practices presented in this book. The Mastermind is made up of leaders like yourself interested in truly being more effective with their leadership. On-line meetings are held once a week for an hour and are facilitated by me. We take each weekly lesson in turn and explore tips, strategies and tactics for integrating and leveraging the lesson into your business and life. To find out more and join the **LEADERSHIP MINDSET MASTERMIND** go to:

https://learn.blainebartlett.com/lmm

A long time ago I made a decision to *be a commitment* to Compassionate Capitalism. The journey for me has been both challenging and rewarding. The challenge has been both internal and external. The internal has been an unbundling and almost clinical examination of what I thought of as truth. It was and is a journey of discovering what to hold on to, what to let go of, and what new to bring in. Paying attention to the questions of what's working and what's not was a useful filter. The external challenges appeared in the form of the very entrenched model of capitalism that we are all familiar with. While much about this economic model is good there is definitely much about it that needs to change. And, as Buckminster Fuller once said, "You never change anything by fighting the existing reality. To change something, build a new model that makes the existing model obsolete." This is what my life is dedicated to and much of the reward comes from having the opportunity to work with individuals like you who believe the challenge is worthy of who they are. Thank you.

ABOUT THE AUTHOR

 **Blaine Bartlett** coaches and consults worldwide with leaders, executives, companies, and governments. He has personally delivered programs to more than a quarter of a million individuals and has directly impacted more than one million people worldwide.

He is featured in the TV series *World's Greatest Motivators* and the movie *Think and Grow Rich: The Legacy.* Blaine is CEO and President of Avatar Resources, Inc., an Adjunct Professor at Beijing University, Managing Director of the Global Coaching Alliance, Founder of the Institute for Compassionate Capitalism, and a longtime member of the Transformational Leadership Council. He sits on the Board of Directors of the Unstoppable Foundation and the World Business Academy where he also serves as Director of Education. In 2012, he was formally invested as a Knight of the Sovereign Order of St. John of Jerusalem Knights of Malta, the world's oldest humanitarian organization.

Blaine is the author of five books – the #1 international best-seller *Compassionate Capitalism: A Journey to the Soul of Business, Discover Your Inner Strength* written in collaboration with Stephen Covey, Ken Blanchard and Brian Tracy, and the best-selling *Three-Dimensional Coaching: Moving Passion into Performance, Tapping into the Soul of Business: The Key to Employee Engagement,* and his newest book, *The Leadership Mindset Weekly.*

Social Media Links

Facebook:	https://www.facebook.com/OfficialBlaineBartlett
LinkedIn:	https://www.linkedin.com/in/blainebartlett
Twitter:	https://twitter.com/blainebartlett
YouTube:	https://www.youtube.com/user/blainebartlett1/playlist
Instagram:	https://www.instagram.com/blainebartlett

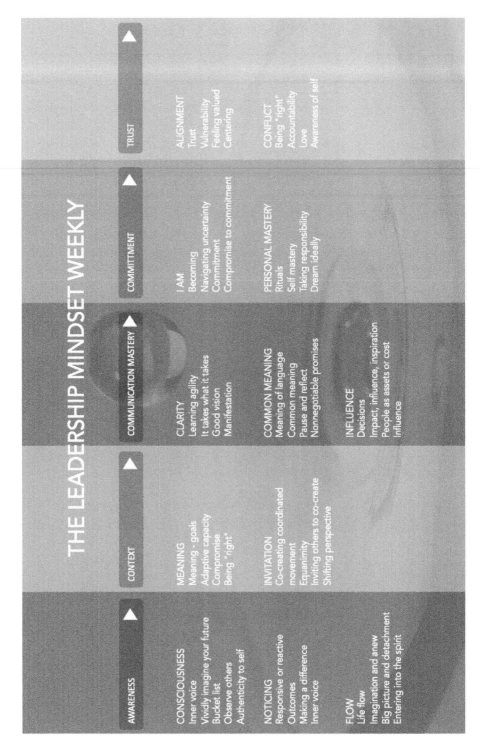

THE LEADERSHIP MINDSET WEEKLY

AWARENESS

CONSCIOUSNESS
Inner voice
Vividly imagine your future
Bucket list
Observe others
Authenticity to self

NOTICING
Responsive or reactive
Outcomes
Making a difference
Inner voice

FLOW
Life flow
Imagination and anew
Big picture and detachment
Entering into the spirit

CONTEXT

MEANING
Meaning - goals
Adaptive capacity
Compromise
Being "right"

INVITATION
Co-creating coordinated movement
Equanimity
Inviting others to co-create
Shifting perspective

COMMUNICATION MASTERY

CLARITY
Learning agility
It takes what it takes
Good vision
Manifestation

COMMON MEANING
Meaning of language
Common meaning
Pause and reflect
Nonnegotiable promises

INFLUENCE
Decisions
Impact, influence, inspiration
People as assets or cost
Influence

COMMITMENT

I AM
Becoming
Navigating uncertainty
Commitment
Compromise to commitment

PERSONAL MASTERY
Rituals
Self mastery
Taking responsibility
Dream ideally

TRUST

ALIGNMENT
Trust
Vulnerability
Feeling valued
Centering

CONFLICT
Being "right"
Accountability
Love
Awareness of self

BlaineBartlett.com

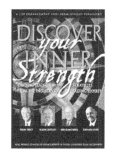

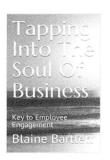

GLENMOORE
PRESS

Made in the USA
Coppell, TX
25 February 2022

74088739R00080